OXFORD BOOKWORMS LIBRARY
Human Interest

Matty Doolin

Stage 2 (700 headwords)

Series Editor: Jennifer Bassett
Founder Editor: Tricia Hedge
Activities Editors: Jennifer Bassett and Alison Baxter

CATHERINE COOKSON

Matty Doolin

Retold by
Diane Mowat

Illustrated by
Chris Molan

OXFORD UNIVERSITY PRESS

OXFORD
UNIVERSITY PRESS

Great Clarendon Street, Oxford OX2 6DP

Oxford University Press is a department of the University of Oxford.
It furthers the University's objective of excellence in research, scholarship,
and education by publishing worldwide in

Oxford New York

Auckland Cape Town Dar es Salaam Hong Kong Karachi
Kuala Lumpur Madrid Melbourne Mexico City Nairobi
New Delhi Shanghai Taipei Toronto

With offices in

Argentina Austria Brazil Chile Czech Republic France Greece
Guatemala Hungary Italy Japan Poland Portugal Singapore
South Korea Switzerland Thailand Turkey Ukraine Vietnam

OXFORD and OXFORD ENGLISH are registered trade marks of
Oxford University Press in the UK and in certain other countries

Word count (main text): 6,580 words

For more information on the Oxford Bookworms Library,
visit www.oup.com/bookworms

CONTENTS

1

Matty and Nelson

'Now, Doolin, what are you going to do?' said Mr Funnell. 'You're fifteen and you're leaving school in three weeks' time. Have you got any plans for a job?'

Matty Doolin looked at his feet. He was a big, strong boy who wasn't afraid of fighting, but he found it difficult to talk. He could never find the right words.

'I don't know, sir. My Dad wants me to get a job in ship-building, like him.'

Mr Funnell was a teacher, but he also helped the children to find jobs when they left school.

Matty could never find the right words.

1

'Well, that's a good job, isn't it?' He waited, but Matty was silent. 'Don't you want to do that, then?'

'No, sir.' Matty's face was unhappy. 'I want . . . I want to work with animals. I've always wanted to do that.'

'Why don't you get a job on a farm?' said Mr Funnell.

'You don't know my Dad, sir.' Now Matty found the words to explain his troubles. 'He says I'm stupid. There are no farms near here and he says I can't go away and live and work on a farm because my Mum says I can't leave home when I'm only fifteen.'

Mr Funnell looked at Matty kindly. 'Well, talk to your parents again. Explain to them how you feel. Then, if they agree, I can help you to find a job on a farm.'

But Matty wasn't very good at explaining his feelings, and he was already in trouble at home because of his dog Nelson, and because of the camping holiday.

The camping holiday was Willie's plan. He, Matty, and Joe were best friends. When school finished, they wanted to go camping in the hills before they all had to begin work. But Matty's parents said that Matty couldn't go.

That Friday afternoon the three boys walked home from school together.

'Can't you ask your Mum and Dad again about the camping?' said Joe. 'Willie and I can't go without you.'

'It's no good,' said Matty. 'They won't listen.'

'It's no good,' said Matty angrily. 'They won't listen. They just say that it's too dangerous for us to go camping in the hills by ourselves. And they're angry with me because of Nelson, too. They say that Nelson's got to go.'

'Why don't you find another home for him?' said Willie. 'He's not really *your* dog, is he? You found him in the street and you've only had him for a few weeks.'

But Joe and Willie didn't understand how Matty felt about animals. Matty really loved Nelson. It was true that Nelson was not a beautiful dog. He was old, had a bad leg, and couldn't see very well in one eye. But he loved Matty as much as Matty loved him. It was also

3

true that he was a noisy dog. When he was in the small back garden, he barked all day long until Matty came home. All the people in the street were very angry about the noise.

And that evening there was more trouble for Matty. When he got in, his mother was waiting for him in the kitchen.

'Just look at what your dog's done now,' she cried angrily. 'I took my eyes off him for ten minutes, and he tried to eat my hat and your father's best shoes! Look!'

Matty looked at the half-eaten things on the table, then at his mother's red, angry face. 'Oh Mum, I'm sorry,' he said. 'But it's only because Nelson's lonely and—'

'He's got to go, Matty! Do you understand? I don't know what your father will say about these shoes.'

Matty knew very well what his father would say. Mr Doolin was a short, heavy man with grey hair and a strong face. He had kind eyes, but he could get angry quickly.

'Right! That's it!' he said when he came home from work. 'That dog leaves the house tomorrow, my boy.'

Matty was sitting by the fire with Nelson at his feet. He put his hand on the dog's head, and decided to say nothing. Perhaps his father would feel differently in the morning. A bit later he tried to ask again about the camping holiday, but the answer was the same. No.

Suddenly Matty got angry. 'I'm nearly sixteen,' he said to his father, 'and I can't go camping, and I can't keep my dog. So don't be surprised if I run away from home!'

'Don't talk to me like that, boy!' his father said.

He took hold of Matty's arm, but Mrs Doolin said quickly, 'There's no need to start a fight. Now come and sit down at the table, both of you, and have your tea.'

*　　*　　*

On Saturday morning Matty got up very early and quietly left the house. He decided to stay out all day. 'If

'*Just look at what your dog's done,*' *Matty's mother cried.*

5

I'm not here,' he thought, 'they can't tell me to take Nelson away. And perhaps by this evening . . .'

He walked round the town, went down to the beach, and went to the cinema. When he got back to his street, it was five o'clock. It was usually very quiet on a Saturday afternoon, but now there were little groups of people there. They were all looking at two men who were shouting. One of the men was Matty's father. What was wrong? His father never shouted at people in the street!

Mrs Doolin looked up at her son.

Suddenly one of the women there saw Matty. 'Ah, poor Matty,' she said.

What was wrong? Was his mother ill?

Matty pushed through the crowd to get to his father.

'You were driving too fast!' Mr Doolin was shouting.

'Look,' the man answered. 'I didn't kill anybody. It was only a dog!'

Then Mr Doolin saw Matty. 'Oh, Matty!' he said. And he put his arm round his son and took him into the house.

Mrs Doolin was sitting at the kitchen table. Her face was in her hands and she was crying. She looked up at her son. 'Oh, Matty!' she said.

'Where is he?' Matty asked.

'Outside.'

Matty turned and ran from the room. Nelson was lying in the garden with blood all over him. His eyes were closed, but he opened them when he heard Matty's voice. Then he tried to get up, but he couldn't move his legs. Matty lay down next to him. He stayed there, and held Nelson's head in his hands until the dog died.

Matty's father pulled him to his feet, but Matty turned and went back into the kitchen. His mother was still crying. 'Oh, Matty,' she said, 'I didn't want Nelson to die like this. I was angry with you because you stayed out all day, and the dog was barking . . . I pushed him out into the street. I'm so sorry, Matty, so sorry.'

She stopped and waited for Matty to speak – but he could say nothing to help her. He went upstairs and lay down on his bed. 'Nelson ran out to look for me,' he thought. 'He didn't see the car, and then . . .'

The door opened and Mr Doolin came in. 'Your mother's very unhappy,' he said quietly. 'She thinks that Nelson died because of her. She carried him back to the house herself. Why didn't you do what we told you to do? Why . . .' Mr Doolin stopped then, because he saw that his son was crying.

Matty did not go to school on Monday, and got into trouble on Tuesday for that. He was silent and unhappy all the time, at home and at school. His mother cooked all his favourite food every day, but Matty wasn't interested.

On the Wednesday of his last week at school, he came home, went in through the back door – and stopped in surprise. The kitchen was full of camping things – on the floor, the table, everywhere. Then he heard a laugh behind the door, and Joe and Mrs Doolin came in.

'Hey, Matty, isn't it exciting?' said Joe happily.

Mrs Doolin looked at her son. 'Are you pleased?'

'Oh, Mum!' Matty said slowly. 'I don't know what to say. It's – it's wonderful! Does – does Dad know?'

'Of course he does!' Mrs Doolin said. 'He came with

The kitchen was full of camping things.

me and Joe – he knew what to buy better than we did.'

And when Mr Doolin came home, he had another present for his son – a camping bucket. Joe stayed for tea, and there was a lot of excited talk about the holiday.

'You're going by train on Saturday,' Mrs Doolin said. 'And you're going to camp on a farm high up in the hills, miles from anywhere. The farmer's a friend of Willie's father, and he'll keep you all out of trouble, I hope.'

Matty put his hand down to touch Nelson under the table. But of course, Nelson wasn't there. 'I forgot!' thought Matty. For a minute he felt unhappy again. He did not want to forget Nelson – ever.

2

Camping

Mr Walsh, the farmer, met the boys at the station. He arrived in an old farm truck, got down from it, and stood and looked at the boys for a minute. Then he said, 'Well, you've arrived.' He wasn't a big man, but he looked very strong. 'Get yourselves into the back of the truck,' he said, 'and don't stand up if you want to arrive in one piece.'

The boys soon understood what he meant. There were no seats in the back of the truck, and Mr Walsh drove

very fast. They were soon falling about everywhere, and they had to hold on to their bags and camping things.

The truck left the town and climbed into the hills. After a while it stopped suddenly, and the boys got down and slowly looked around. On their left there were fields with stone walls round them, and on their right, a big white house and the farm buildings.

'Well, this is your field,' said Mr Walsh. 'Bring your things and follow me.' He went through a gate into the nearest field, and the boys hurried after him.

'Put your tents here,' Mr Walsh said. 'This is a good place.' He looked at the three boys, one by one, then spoke to Matty. 'Three things to remember, right?

'This is your field,' said Mr Walsh.

Always shut gates behind you. Don't light fires in the woods. And no noise or shouting after ten o'clock at night. Now, put your tents up and then come to the house to get some milk. And perhaps Mrs Walsh will have some tea for you.'

And for the first time, he smiled. Then he walked away.

'I like the sound of that tea,' said Willie happily. 'But he wasn't very friendly at first, was he?'

'Come on,' said Matty. 'Let's get these tents up.'

The boys worked hard, and soon they were walking across to the farmhouse and knocking on the door. A girl of about twelve years old opened it. She had a round face, laughing grey-green eyes, and long brown hair. 'They're here, Mum,' she called.

A small, kind-looking woman came to the door.

The boys worked hard.

'Come in,' she said, in a soft, slow voice. She asked the boys their names, then turned to her daughter. 'This is Jessica,' she said. 'Now, sit down, and we'll get you some tea.'

It was a large farmhouse tea, and the hungry boys ate nearly everything on the table. When they finished, they thanked Mrs Walsh and left the house to go back to their field. Jessica went with them, and talked and laughed with Joe and Willie.

Matty wasn't very pleased about this. 'Girls are always trouble,' he thought. He felt angry, and when Jessica took Joe and Willie to show them the stream, Matty stayed behind at the tents. 'I'm not running after a girl!' he said to himself. But suddenly he felt very alone.

When the others came back, they didn't bring any water with them. 'Forgot to take the bucket,' said Willie.

'You're a fine camper!' said Matty crossly. 'I'll get it myself.' He took the bucket and began to walk across the field to find the stream. Then he heard someone behind him, and Jessica ran up.

'I'll show you the best place to get drinking water,' she said. She ran past him down the hill and Matty followed.

The stream ran quickly, falling down over rocks, talking and laughing to itself. The water was bright and silvery in the sunlight, and on the other side of the stream

Matty just stood and looked at it.

were tall green plants with purple flowers. Matty just stood and looked at it. 'How beautiful it is!' he thought. 'I'd like to stay here for ever.' He looked up at the hills all around him, and the mountains behind. Then he remembered the ship-building job which was waiting for him. There are no streams or hills or mountains in the town.

Suddenly, he saw Jessica, higher up the stream. She was watching his face with interest.

14

'It's wonderful, this place,' he said slowly. 'I've never seen anything like it.'

'It gets very cold in winter,' said Jessica. 'Your fingers turn blue and fall off.'

Matty smiled. 'Well, you've still got ten of them.'

*   *   *

That first night the boys could not get to sleep. Outside the tents everything was dark and silent. In a town there is always some noise, and this lonely field high in the hills was too quiet for them. But they were tired, and in the end they fell asleep.

The next morning they cooked their breakfast over a fire, and then went up to the farm to get some milk. Mr Walsh was standing outside the cow shed. 'Would you like to see round the farm?' he asked.

'Would you like to see round the farm?'

'Oh, yes please,' said Joe and Willie.

Mr Walsh finished milking the cows, and then he walked round the farm with the boys. He showed them all the animals and explained all the work of the farm. Matty listened carefully to every word, but it was Joe and Willie who asked most of the questions. Suddenly, Mr Walsh turned to Matty, and said, 'You haven't got much to say.'

'Oh, Matty's always quiet, Mr Walsh,' said Joe.

Matty didn't like it when people talked about him. He turned his head away and looked across at another building. Then, 'Oh, look!' he cried. 'You've got dogs!'

'You've got dogs!'

'Of course we've got dogs,' said Mr Walsh. 'This is a sheep farm. You can't keep sheep on these hills without dogs to help you.'

The two sheep dogs came up to the boys. Joe and Willie tried to make friends with them, but the bigger dog wasn't interested. Matty just stood and watched; then the bigger dog came over to Matty and looked up at him. Matty slowly and lovingly stroked its ears.

'That's Betsy,' Mr Walsh said. 'She's seven – and that's her son, Prince.' He watched Matty. 'That's strange. Betsy doesn't usually like people touching her.'

'I like dogs.' Matty's voice was soft, and he went on stroking the dog's ears.

'Matty loves dogs!' Joe said. 'That's why we're here. His dog was killed by a car, and it was his mother who—'

'It wasn't my mother!' Matty said angrily.

'All right, all right! There's no need to get angry, boy,' said Mr Walsh. 'Off you go now. I've got work to do.'

3

Blisters and storms

When they got back to their camp, the boys decided to go for their first long walk. They took some food and water, and went off along the road, laughing and talking.

By four o'clock they were tired, hot, thirsty, and hungry – and Willie had a big blister on his foot. He could only walk very slowly, and he wanted to sit down and rest all the time. 'It really hurts,' he said unhappily to the others.

'Put your shoe back on, Willie,' said Matty. 'You can't walk with only one shoe.'

'It really hurts.'

Suddenly Joe cried out excitedly, 'Look! Look what's coming up behind us! It's Mr Walsh's truck!'

In a few minutes the truck came up to them and stopped. Mr Walsh looked down at them. There was a smile in his

eyes. 'You're all half dead, your feet hurt, and you'll never do it again,' he said.

They explained about Willie's blister, so Mr Walsh took them back with him in the truck. He dropped Matty and Joe by the field, but took Willie back to the farm. 'Mrs Walsh will put something on that foot for you,' he said.

Matty and Joe were not very happy about this. 'We've only got old bread and cold meat for our tea,' said Joe, 'and Mrs Walsh will give Willie something nice and hot.'

And when Willie came back much later, full of Mrs Walsh's good food, his friends were not pleased. There were a few angry words, but by the next morning, after a good breakfast, they all forgot about it.

They couldn't go for a walk that day because of Willie's foot, so they went back to the farm. Matty wasn't sure about this at first. He felt that Mr Walsh was always looking at him strangely, but the others didn't want to go without him.

When they got there, Mr Walsh was busy. Matty was happy just looking at all the animals, but Joe and Willie were soon bored. They couldn't stay in the same place for more than a minute, and after a while Mr Walsh came up to them. 'Do you boys want a job to do?' he asked.

'Oh yes, yes,' they all answered quickly.

'You can work on the heap.'

'You'll get dirty, but you can get washed after,' said Mr Walsh. 'Over there you'll find some long forks, and you can work on the heap.'

'You mean the manure heap?' said Joe.

'That's right. You have to turn it over. It's smelly, but it won't hurt you.' Mr Walsh smiled quietly to himself.

Later, when they were washing their clothes in the stream, Joe said, 'That's the last time I'll do that.'

'Oh, it was all right,' said Matty. 'I enjoyed it. It's only smelly if you think it is.'

His friends looked at him, their mouths open in surprise.

* * *

In the afternoon it got very hot, and Jessica came down to the field to tell them that a storm was coming. 'My father says that it's going to be a bad one. Get your things inside the tents now,' she said.

While they were moving their things into the tents, the light suddenly changed. The sky went black and everything was very quiet and still. The boys sat together in one of the tents, and waited.

Suddenly there was a great crash of thunder. Lightning shot from the sky and filled the tent with light. The boys

Lightning shot from the sky.

21

sat there, afraid to move. Then the thunder crashed again, and again – louder and more terrible each time. Willie was white and shaking. 'It'll be all right when it rains,' Matty said. 'Listen! Here it is now.'

But it wasn't just rain. Rivers of water fell from the sky and it got worse and worse. They couldn't talk because of the noise of the rain. Then Joe looked up and saw that the sides of the tent were wet – on the inside. Soon the rain was coming in everywhere and their clothes, food, sleeping bags got wetter and wetter. 'It can't go on for ever,' Matty said. But the rain didn't stop, and an hour later their tent fell down on top of

Soon the rain was coming in everywhere.

them. The three boys lay there, with their wet things all around them, feeling very unhappy.

At last help came, and they heard the sound of Mr Walsh's voice above the noise of the storm. 'Come on! Get out of there!' he shouted. He pulled them out one by one, and they followed him through the driving rain back to the farm. 'Get in there!' Mr Walsh said, and the boys found themselves in a warm, dry, comfortable barn. Then Mrs Walsh brought them a hot drink and some dry clothes, and they lay down to sleep. But they remembered that storm all their lives.

Mr Walsh woke them the next morning. 'Come on!' he shouted. 'Are you going to sleep all day? Here's some tea. Drink that, and then go and put your things out to dry.'

It was a bright sunny morning. The boys went back to their camp, put the tent up again, and put everything out to dry in the sun.

A little later Mr Walsh came down to the field. 'Would you like to see the sheep dogs at work?' he asked the boys.

'Oh, yes!' said Matty excitedly. 'I'd love that.'

But Joe and Willie didn't want to go, so Matty and Mr Walsh went off together. The two dogs came running from the hills behind the farm, and began to follow them. Betsy walked just behind Mr Walsh, with Prince behind

her. Matty tried to stroke Betsy, but Betsy moved away and Mr Walsh had to call her back. 'Never do that,' he said to Matty. 'Not when a dog is working.'

They walked for miles, high up into the mountains. Then they stopped, and Matty saw sheep on the far side of the valley. The dogs lay at Mr Walsh's feet, waiting.

'Away, girl,' Mr Walsh said to Betsy. And Betsy shot off down the hill and up the far side of the valley. A minute later, Prince followed, going round the other side of the sheep. Mr Walsh whistled once, twice, and together the two dogs drove the sheep down into the valley, through a gate, and into another field.

Matty watched silently, afraid to say anything because he didn't want Mr Walsh to be angry with him again. But he loved every minute of it.

When they were near the farm again, Mr Walsh

The two dogs drove the sheep down into the valley.

turned to Matty and said, 'What are you going to do when you leave school? Find work in the town?'

'Yes. Ship-building,' said Matty, sounding unhappy. He was afraid to explain to Mr Walsh what he really wanted. 'If I tell him that I want to work with animals, he'll just laugh at me,' Matty thought. So he said nothing.

When he got back, Willie and Joe were sitting by the tents. They didn't look very happy.

'What's the matter?' Matty asked them.

'We're bored,' Joe said.

'Yes,' said Willie. 'There are no towns near here, and you've got to walk for miles to get anywhere.'

Matty couldn't understand it. They had two weeks of holiday. It was only Tuesday of the first week, and his friends were bored already. He just couldn't understand it.

4

Helping on the farm

By Saturday Joe and Willie wanted to go home. But Mr Walsh came down to see them. 'I'm going into town today,' he said. 'Do you want to come with me?'

'Oh yes!' Joe and Willie shouted.

But Matty said, 'I'd like to stay here, if that's all right.'

'Yes, if you want to,' Mr Walsh said. He gave Matty a long look. 'You're a strange boy.'

Matty said nothing, but after Mr Walsh left with Jessica and the two boys, he went to find Mrs Walsh.

He worked hard, and enjoyed it all.

'Can I help you on the farm today?' he asked. 'I'll do anything. I'll turn some more of the manure heap, if you like.'

Mrs Walsh looked at him, and smiled. 'Come and have a cup of coffee with me,' she said, 'and then we'll begin.'

So Matty spent his first real day on a farm. He worked hard, and enjoyed it all, even the dirty, smelly jobs. He turned the manure heap, cleaned out the cow shed, and took food to the pigs. Later, he helped Mrs Walsh with the milking, and he learnt the names of the seven cows. He had lunch and tea with Mrs Walsh in the kitchen, and he felt really happy. For him, it was a wonderful day.

Joe and Willie enjoyed their day in town too, but on Sunday it rained, and they were bored and cross.

On Monday evening it rained again. 'That's it!' said Willie. 'I've had enough! Matty, let's go home tomorrow.'

'You can do what you like, Willie,' Matty said, 'but I'm staying until the end of our holiday. What about you, Joe?'

But Joe agreed with Willie.

*   *   *

Joe and Willie didn't go home the next day. They planned to, but they were just finishing breakfast when somebody walked up the field from the stream. It was Mr Funnell, their teacher from school! He saw them and stopped. 'Well!' he cried. 'I didn't know that you liked camping!'

'What are you doing here, sir?' the boys asked, surprised.

'Oh, I often come here. I know this place well,' Mr Funnell replied. 'Mr Walsh is an old friend, and I love walking in these hills. Are you enjoying camping here?'

'Well, sir,' said Joe. 'It's a bit different from the town, and we're . . . we're a bit bored.'

'What about you, Doolin?' Mr Funnell asked.

'I've enjoyed every minute of it, sir,' said Matty.

'Well, I'm going to have breakfast with Mr Walsh now,' Mr Funnell said. 'I'll come and see you later.'

He left, and Willie said, 'Well, we can't leave now!'

Matty tried to feel pleased that his friends were staying. 'I'd really like to go for a long walk with Mr Funnell,' he thought, 'but he'll never ask me, with Joe and Willie here.'

Matty was wrong. Mr Funnell did ask him to go for a walk in the hills – but he asked Joe and Willie too, and Mr Walsh and Jessica came with them. Joe and Willie talked and laughed with Jessica, but Matty didn't say much. He was enjoying just looking at the hills and mountains.

Matty saw that Mr Walsh was looking at him strangely.

At the top of one high hill they stopped to look around them. Mr Funnell turned to Matty. 'Do you like it up here in these hills?' he asked.

'Oh yes, sir. I think it's wonderful,' said Matty.

'But only for a summer holiday, is that right?'

'Oh no. I'd like to be here every day, summer or winter.' Matty saw that Mr Walsh was looking at him strangely. 'He doesn't like me,' Matty thought, and he turned and walked over to Jessica and his friends. They were all sitting high up on a rock.

'Are you afraid of being high up?' Jessica asked him.

'No, I'm not,' Matty answered. 'Are you?'

'Me? Of course I'm not. I've been nearly to the top of the little mountain behind our house, and that's very dangerous. I'm sure you couldn't do that.'

'Perhaps I couldn't,' Matty replied. He turned away from her. 'She's like her father,' he thought. 'She doesn't like me, and she thinks I'm stupid.'

They all went back to the farm for tea. Later, Mr Walsh said, 'I have to go into town again tomorrow. I'm taking some sheep to market. Would you boys like to come?'

Of course, Joe and Willie said yes, but Matty said, 'If it's all right with you, sir, I'd like to stay on the farm.'

Mr Walsh gave him another strange look, and Matty felt uncomfortable. 'Why don't I keep quiet?' he thought.

That evening Mr Funnell had a few words alone with Matty. 'Listen, Matty,' he said. 'Talk to Mr Walsh a bit more. Tell him about yourself. Tell him how you love animals. Remember, if you want something in this life, you have to work to get it. Do you understand?'

Matty understood very well, but talking was so difficult. He could never find the right words to say.

5

A night on the hills

The next morning there were dark storm clouds in the sky when Mr Walsh put the last sheep into the truck and pushed Joe and Willie up with them. Prince jumped in too, Mr Funnell got into the front, and then they were ready to go. Mr Walsh turned and looked hard at Matty.

'Right. Get to work, then,' he said, with a half smile. 'You said that you wanted to stay here and work, didn't you? So, you're the farmer for today. And when I come back, I'll want to see that everything's all right.'

Matty didn't understand this. 'Why did he say that?' he thought. 'He doesn't mean it – he's just laughing at me.'

The truck drove away, and Mrs Walsh and Jessica looked at Matty. Mrs Walsh smiled.

'Well,' she said. 'There's a lot to do. Why don't you begin in the cow shed? I've got work to do in the house.'

So Matty began in the cow shed. He enjoyed the work very much, but Jessica followed him around, asking questions all the time. Where do you live? How old is your mother? What is your father called? What did you like best in school? Do you like Mr Funnell? How much money will you get in a ship-building job? When Matty told her the answer to that question, she was very surprised. 'That's much more than you get when you work on a farm,' she said. Then she asked, 'Have you got a girlfriend?'

'What do I want with a girlfriend?' Matty said angrily.

Jessica moved away from him. 'Why are you always so cross and unfriendly?' she said, in a small voice. 'You never say anything nice to anybody, do you?'

She walked away, and Matty watched her unhappily. He wanted to call her back, but he knew that he didn't have the right words.

*   *   *

It was about three o'clock when Matty, who was working in the barn, heard the storm in the hills. It was still a long way away, but he could hear it clearly. Just then someone called him – 'Matty! Matty!'

He ran from the barn. Mrs Walsh was standing outside the kitchen door and he hurried over to her. There was a man with her, and she said quickly, 'This is one of my brothers, Matty. My other brother is very ill, and we have to go to him now. Have you seen Jessica?'

'No, Mrs Walsh. Not for some time.'

'I think she's up the mountain at the back of the house. She was angry about something at lunch-time, and she always goes up there when she's angry. If she isn't back soon, send Betsy to get her. Just say, "Fetch . . . Fetch Jessica." Betsy will find her.' Mrs Walsh stopped and looked up at the sky. 'No, get her now,' she said. 'There's a storm coming. Will you do that for me?'

'Yes, of course, Mrs Walsh,' said Matty. 'I'll go now.'

Mrs Walsh hurried away to her brother's car. Matty called to Betsy, who jumped up immediately and followed him. They went round to the back of the farm and Matty looked up at the hills. Already the mist was coming down quickly, and he could see very little.

'Fetch . . . Fetch Jessica,' he said to the dog, and at once Betsy began to run fast up the hill.

Matty watched her, but a few minutes later the cold, wet mist was all around him, and he could see nothing.

He began to shake with cold, so he ran to the camp and put on a pullover and a raincoat. Then he hurried back to the bottom of the hill and began to call Jessica's name. He called for half an hour, but Jessica and Betsy did not come. Matty was afraid. He knew that they were in trouble.

He put on a pullover and a raincoat.

33

He decided to go and look for them, and began to climb quickly up the steep hillside, through a white wall of mist. Every few minutes he stopped, put his hands to his mouth and shouted Jessica's name. But everywhere was silent, and Matty felt very alone.

Higher up the mist was thinner, and when he got to the top, he stopped to rest and look round. But it wasn't the top! All around him, everywhere, there were more mountains, higher and higher. How could he find her here? 'Jessica! Jessica!' he shouted. But there was no reply.

Suddenly the mist came down again, colder and wetter than ever. 'I must go back,' thought Matty, afraid. 'I'll never find my way in this.' But which way was back? He moved slowly and carefully, but the mist hid everything and once he nearly fell down some steep rocks. After that, he moved on his hands and knees.

Then, somewhere in front of him, Matty heard a bark.

After that, he moved on his hands and knees.

Betsy! Carefully, he moved nearer to the sound. Betsy barked again and Matty stopped. Just in time! Below him the rock fell away into nothing. He looked down. Betsy was lying on a narrow ledge about a foot below him. One of her legs was under a heavy rock, and she couldn't move.

'Quiet, Betsy. Quiet,' Matty said. He lay down and held on to the dog with one hand. With the other, he pushed the rock from her leg. Then he pulled her up on to her three feet, and, with one last pull, she was beside him. She licked Matty's face, and then began to lick her leg.

Matty could see that the leg was broken, but Betsy stood up and began to walk on three legs. Then she stopped and turned to look at Matty. Her eyes were saying, 'Come on.'

The mist moved away again and Matty followed Betsy along a steep path. After a time he began to call again, 'Jessica! Jessica!' And at last, he heard something.

'Oooo! Oooo!'

'That's her, Betsy!' he shouted excitedly. 'Find her!'

Matty could see that Betsy's leg was hurting, but she didn't stop. Every few seconds Matty called Jessica's name, and each time the answer was nearer. And then, suddenly, he saw her! She was standing on a rock above him, and the next minute she was beside him.

'Oh, Matty!' she cried. And then she saw Betsy. 'Oh, no! Her leg's broken. Oh, Betsy, I'm sorry! I'm sorry!'

Then Jessica looked at Matty. 'I heard you when you called me, but I didn't answer,' she said. 'I just moved away and waited for you to find me. But you didn't, and then I got afraid and began to run. And now I'm lost.'

'But *why* didn't you answer me?' Matty asked.

'I was angry because you didn't want to talk to me this morning . . . and it gets so lonely in the holidays.' She began to cry. 'And now we're lost! I'm sorry, Matty!'

'Don't cry,' said Matty. 'Everything'll be all right. Betsy will take us home.'

But Betsy could no longer stand. She was lying under a rock, with her head on the ground. Only her eyes moved when she looked up at them.

It was now raining hard. Jessica was only wearing a thin summer dress and she was shaking with cold. Matty took off his raincoat and gave it to her. 'Let's sit against this rock with Betsy,' he said. 'We won't get so wet then.'

The rain drove into their faces and they got wetter and wetter. For a while they called for help, but nobody came, and after half an hour they stopped shouting.

Then Matty said, 'When your mother and father get back, they'll come and find us. We'll be home soon.'

'These storms can go on all night, and they'll never

Matty took her hand. It felt very cold.

find us in all this rain and mist.' Jessica was nearly crying again, and Matty took her hand. It felt very cold.

'Look,' said Matty, worried. 'Put my pullover on too. Here. Push your legs into the arms of the pullover and pull it up under the raincoat. It'll help to keep you warm.'

'But what about you?' said Jessica. 'You'll get so cold.'

'My shirt's already wet, so it doesn't matter,' said Matty. 'Now, lie down with your back against Betsy's back. She's nice and warm. I'll lie on your other side, and you'll soon feel warmer.'

It began to get dark. Matty lay with his back against Jessica, and the rain ran in rivers through his thin shirt and trousers. He felt too tired to shout any more. 'Will I ever see my mother again?' he thought. Soon he no longer felt cold, only sleepy.

6

A new life for Matty

It was two o'clock in the morning when help came, but Matty remembered very little about it. He just wanted to go on sleeping. And when he next woke up, he was lying in a bed with bright sunshine all around him. Then he saw Mrs Walsh's face above him, and suddenly remembered.

'Jessica?' he said.

'She's all right. She's all right.' Mrs Walsh's voice was shaking, and she was crying and smiling at the same time. 'Don't you want to see who's here?' she said.

Matty turned his head. His mother was sitting beside the bed. 'Oh, Matty,' she said, 'we nearly lost you!' She took his hand, and went on softly, 'But you're all right, and that's all that matters. And Matty, I want you to know something. Your dad and I agree that you can do what you like with your life. The most important thing is that you're all right. So you can take Mr Walsh's job.'

'Job? What job?'

'He planned to ask you at the end of your holiday,' said Mrs Doolin. 'He needs help on the farm, and he likes you. He says that you're a good worker, and you don't talk all the time, like your friends.'

Matty's mouth fell open with surprise, and just then Mr Walsh came in, with Matty's father.

'Hello, boy,' said Mr Doolin. 'You've had a bit of an adventure, haven't you? But you did well, boy, you did well.' He turned away, looking uncomfortable and pleased at the same time.

'You did well, boy.'

Then Mr Walsh spoke. 'You knew the right things to do up on the mountain, and you did them,' he said. 'Jessica's told us all about it. Now you do what Mrs Walsh and your mother say. I want to see you well before you begin to work on the farm. Do you understand?'

Matty found his voice. 'Yes,' he said.

'You'll have to work hard, you know. Sixteen hours a day sometimes. All right?'

'Yes,' Matty said again.

'That's all right then. Your mother and father agree, but your mother wants to see you at home every other weekend. Now go to sleep again and get well.'

The next time Matty woke up, Joe and Willie were sitting by the bed.

'Are you all right?' Joe said. 'You nearly died, you know. And you're famous now! The newspapers said that it's because of you that Jessica and the dog are alive.'

'Betsy!' Matty said. 'How is she?'

'Her foot's broken, but she'll be all right,' Willie said. 'Are you going to stay on the farm, Matty?'

'Yes, I am,' said Matty happily.

'Well, we'll come and see you,' said Joe.

'But not to stay,' said Willie, laughing. 'Me and Joe, we're town people. And I'm never going camping again!'

When they left, Matty lay back and thought happily about the new life in front of him. 'It all began because

40

Matty thought happily about the new life in front of him.

of Nelson,' he thought. 'And one day I'm going to get a dog, a dog that belongs to me alone, and call him Nelson. We'll go all over these hills and mountains together, mist or no mist – and we'll always find our way home.'

GLOSSARY

bark *(v)* to make the sound that a dog makes

blister a sore place on your foot made by shoes that are too big or too small

camping living and sleeping in tents for a short time

clean *(v)* to take dirt away from something

farm the fields and buildings for keeping animals and growing food

fetch to go and get someone or something

lick to move the tongue along something

lightning a sudden bright light in the sky during a storm

mist a kind of thin cloud near the ground

path a narrow way for people to walk on

sir a polite word for a man

steep when ground gets higher very quickly, e.g. a steep hill

stroke *(v)* to move your hand softly across something, again and again

thunder a loud noise in the sky when there is a storm

valley low land, usually with a river, between hills or mountains

whistle *(v)* to blow through a small gap between your lips, to make a high sound

Matty Doolin

ACTIVITIES

Before Reading

1 Read the story introduction on the first page of the book, and the back cover. How much do you know now about the story? Tick one of the boxes.

	YES	NO
1 Matty lives with his parents.	☐	☐
2 He left school a few weeks ago.	☐	☐
3 Matty's father works on a farm.	☐	☐
4 Matty wants to get a job in ship-building.	☐	☐
5 He wants to go on a camping holiday with his friends Willie and Joe.	☐	☐
6 Matty's dog Nelson is a good, quiet dog.	☐	☐
7 Matty loves Nelson very much.	☐	☐
8 Matty is in trouble because of Nelson.	☐	☐

2 **Matty wants to get a job on a farm. Why can't he do this? Choose the best answer.**

1 He wants to stay with his friends.

2 His father has a job in ship-building.

3 He lives in a town with no farms and he is too young to leave home.

4 His mother doesn't like his dog.

3 Can you guess what happens in this story? Tick one of the boxes each time.

		YES	NO
1	Matty goes camping with his friends.	☐	☐
2	He doesn't enjoy the holiday.	☐	☐
3	He gets a job in ship-building.	☐	☐
4	He gets a job on a farm.	☐	☐
5	He works with animals, but not on a farm.	☐	☐
6	He leaves home with Nelson and begins a new life.	☐	☐
7	Nelson dies and Matty is very unhappy.	☐	☐

4 What kind of jobs would you like? Choose answers to these questions and explain why you would like or wouldn't like these jobs.

1 Would you like to work with
  a) children?   c) computers?
  b) animals?   d) sick people?

2 Would you like a job
  a) near your family?   d) on a ship?
  b) in a different country?   e) on a farm?
  c) in an office?   f) in a theatre?

3 Would you like to be
  a) a doctor?   c) a footballer?
  b) a pilot?   d) a teacher?

While Reading

Read Chapter 1, then answer these questions.

Who

1 . . . said Matty was stupid?
2 . . . wanted to help Matty find a job on a farm?
3 . . . talked about running away from home?
4 . . . pushed Matty's dog out into the street?
5 . . . cried when Nelson died?
6 . . . went to buy all the camping things?

Read Chapter 2, then answer these questions.

1 What three things did Mr Walsh tell the boys to do?
2 Why couldn't the boys get to sleep on the first night?
3 Who asked Mr Walsh a lot of questions about the farm?
4 Why was Mr Walsh surprised when Matty stroked Betsy's ears?

Read Chapter 3. Here are some untrue sentences about the chapter. Change them into true sentences.

1 Willie and Joe enjoyed working on the manure heap.
2 In the storm the boys' tent stayed up.

3 For the rest of the night the boys slept in the farmhouse.

4 When Matty went with Mr Walsh to watch the sheep dogs at work, he was bored.

5 Matty told Mr Walsh he wanted to work with animals.

Read Chapter 4. Who said this, and to whom?

1 'You're a strange boy.'

2 'I've had enough!'

3 'I'd like to be here every day, summer or winter.'

4 'Remember, if you want something in this life, you have to work to get it.'

Read Chapter 5, and complete these sentences.

1 Matty thought that Jessica asked too many _____.

2 Jessica thought that Matty was _____ and _____.

3 Matty called Betsy and said, '_____ Jessica.'

4 On the mountain the _____ hid everything.

5 Jessica got very cold, so Matty gave her his _____ and his _____.

Before you read Chapter 6 (*A new life for Matty*), can you guess what happens? Tick one of the boxes.

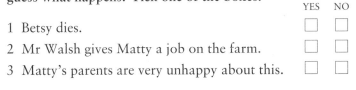

	YES	NO
1 Betsy dies.	☐	☐
2 Mr Walsh gives Matty a job on the farm.	☐	☐
3 Matty's parents are very unhappy about this.	☐	☐

After Reading

1 **On Tuesday Willie wrote a postcard to his mother. Use these words to complete it. (Use each word once.)**

blister, camping, enjoyed, forks, happy, heap, job, lightning, smelly, storm, tent, thunder, walk, wet

Dear Mum, I don't think I like _____ holidays! When we went for a _____, I got a _____ on my foot. Then Mr Walsh gave us a _____ to do on the farm. We worked on the manure _____ and turned it over with _____. It was really dirty and _____, but Matty _____ it! And yesterday we had a terrible _____. There was _____ and _____, and it rained and rained. Everything got _____ and our _____ fell down! I'll be _____ to get back home! Love, Willie

2 **Match these halves of sentences to tell the story of Matty's and Jessica's adventure on the hills.**

1 When Betsy and Jessica did not come back,

2 He shouted Jessica's name into the mist,

3 After a time he heard a bark and found Betsy,

4 Betsy then helped him to find Jessica,

5 Betsy could not take them home

6 By now Matty and Jessica were very cold and wet

7 They were too tired to shout any more,

8 who was lying on a ledge with a broken leg.

9 because she could no longer stand on her broken leg.

10 Matty decided to climb the hill and look for them.

11 so they lay down next to Betsy to keep warm.

12 but Jessica was lost too and didn't know the way home.

13 and Mr Walsh did not find them until many hours later.

14 but there was no answer.

3 **Here are Mr Funnell and Mr Walsh, having a talk about Matty. Write out their conversation in the correct order and put in the speakers' names. Mr Funnell speaks first (3).**

1 _____ 'No, he hasn't. He told me that he's getting a job in the town, in ship-building.'

2 _____ 'Yes, he's a good worker. And I need help here.'

3 _____ 'What do you think of young Matty Doolin? Do you like him?'

4 _____ 'He wants to work with animals, you know. Has he said anything to you about that?'

5 _____ 'Yes, I will. I'll ask him at the end of the holiday.'

6 _____ 'His father wants him to do that, but Matty wants to work on a farm. Will he be good at it?'

7 _____ 'Yes, I do. He doesn't talk all the time, like his friends. The dogs like him, too.'

8 _____ 'Will you give him a job, then?'

4 Here is a new illustration for the story. Find the best place
in the story to put the picture, and answer these questions.

The picture goes on page _____.

1 Who are the people in this picture?

2 Where are they, and what is the boy doing?

3 Why is the boy angry?

Now write a caption for the illustration.

Caption: _____

5 **What do you think about Matty and his new job? Do you agree (A) or disagree (D) with these sentences?**

1 At fifteen, Matty was too young to leave home.
2 He was not too young to leave home, because Mr and Mrs Walsh will be like second parents to him.
3 At fifteen, nobody really knows what they want to do. Matty will be bored with his job after a few years.
4 Matty will be very happy in his job, because he loves animals and he loves the hills and mountains.
5 Farm work is very hard. Sometimes it is sixteen hours a day, seven days a week, and Matty won't like it.

6 **In his first winter Matty writes a letter to his mother. Use the words below to write his letter for him.**

- *farm work hard / work long hours / really enjoy it*
- *always hungry / eat a lot*
- *Mrs Walsh's cooking / wonderful / very happy*
- *Mr and Mrs Walsh / very kind / Jessica and I / good friends / my best friend / Betsy!*

7 **Here are some new titles for the story. Which titles do you like? Can you explain why?**

A Camping Holiday   A Mountain Adventure
A Dog Called Nelson   Betsy
Matty Gets his Wish   Matty Finds a Job

ABOUT THE AUTHOR

Catherine Cookson's real name was Catherine Ann McMullen. She was born in 1906 in Tyneside, in the north-east of England. Her family was very poor. She never knew her father, and she lived with her mother and grandmother. She left school at thirteen, and her first job was as a servant. Later, she moved to Hastings in the south of England and married a teacher.

She began to write when she was forty years old. Most of her books are set in the north-east of England in the 1800s and early 1900s, and are about the everyday lives of poor, working people. They show how hard life was for poor people at that time. Some of her books are series, for example, the 'Mary Ann' and the 'Tilly Trotter' titles, and many of her stories are now also television plays.

Catherine Cookson's books for younger readers show the same understanding of life as her adult books. Things do not come easily, but life can sometimes be kind if we keep trying. Her children's books include *Mrs Flannagan's Trumpet*, *Lanky Jones*, and *Our John Willie*.

During her life Catherine Cookson wrote nearly a hundred books, and she sold nearly 100 million copies all over the world. In 1985 she received an OBE, and in 1993 the Queen made her a Dame of the British Empire because her books were so popular. She died in 1998.

OXFORD BOOKWORMS LIBRARY

Classics • Crime & Mystery • Factfiles • Fantasy & Horror
Human Interest • Playscripts • Thriller & Adventure
True Stories • World Stories

The OXFORD BOOKWORMS LIBRARY provides enjoyable reading in English, with a wide range of classic and modern fiction, non-fiction, and plays. It includes original and adapted texts in seven carefully graded language stages, which take learners from beginner to advanced level. An overview is given on the next pages.

All Stage 1 titles are available as audio recordings, as well as over eighty other titles from Starter to Stage 6. All Starters and many titles at Stages 1 to 4 are specially recommended for younger learners. Every Bookworm is illustrated, and Starters and Factfiles have full-colour illustrations.

The OXFORD BOOKWORMS LIBRARY also offers extensive support. Each book contains an introduction to the story, notes about the author, a glossary, and activities. Additional resources include tests and worksheets, and answers for these and for the activities in the books. There is advice on running a class library, using audio recordings, and the many ways of using Oxford Bookworms in reading programmes. Resource materials are available on the website <www.oup.com/bookworms>.

The *Oxford Bookworms Collection* is a series for advanced learners. It consists of volumes of short stories by well-known authors, both classic and modern. Texts are not abridged or adapted in any way, but carefully selected to be accessible to the advanced student.

You can find details and a full list of titles in the *Oxford Bookworms Library Catalogue* and *Oxford English Language Teaching Catalogues*, and on the website <www.oup.com/bookworms>.

THE OXFORD BOOKWORMS LIBRARY
GRADING AND SAMPLE EXTRACTS

STARTER • 250 HEADWORDS

present simple – present continuous – imperative –
can/cannot, must – *going to* (future) – simple gerunds …

Her phone is ringing – but where is it?

Sally gets out of bed and looks in her bag. No phone. She looks under the bed. No phone. Then she looks behind the door. There is her phone. Sally picks up her phone and answers it. *Sally's Phone*

STAGE 1 • 400 HEADWORDS

… past simple – coordination with *and*, *but*, *or* –
subordination with *before, after, when, because, so* …

I knew him in Persia. He was a famous builder and I worked with him there. For a time I was his friend, but not for long. When he came to Paris, I came after him – I wanted to watch him. He was a very clever, very dangerous man. *The Phantom of the Opera*

STAGE 2 • 700 HEADWORDS

… present perfect – *will* (future) – *(don't) have to, must not, could* –
comparison of adjectives – simple *if* clauses – past continuous –
tag questions – *ask/tell* + infinitive …

While I was writing these words in my diary, I decided what to do. I must try to escape. I shall try to get down the wall outside. The window is high above the ground, but I have to try. I shall take some of the gold with me – if I escape, perhaps it will be helpful later. *Dracula*

Of course, it was most important that no one should see Colin, Mary, or Dickon entering the secret garden. So Colin gave orders to the gardeners that they must all keep away from that part of the garden in future. *The Secret Garden*

I was glad. Now Hyde could not show his face to the world again. If he did, every honest man in London would be proud to report him to the police. *Dr Jekyll and Mr Hyde*

If he had spoken Estella's name, I would have hit him. I was so angry with him, and so depressed about my future, that I could not eat the breakfast. Instead I went straight to the old house. *Great Expectations*

When I stepped up to the piano, I was confident. It was as if I knew that the prodigy side of me really did exist. And when I started to play, I was so caught up in how lovely I looked that I didn't worry how I would sound. *The Joy Luck Club*

The Piano

ROSEMARY BORDER

One day, a farmer tells a farm boy to take everything out of an old building and throw it away. 'It's all rubbish,' he says.

In the middle of all the rubbish, the boy finds a beautiful old piano. He has never played before, but now, when his fingers touch the piano, he begins to play. He closes his eyes and the music comes to him – and the music moves his fingers.

When he opens his eyes again, he knows that his life is changed for ever . . .

Huckleberry Finn

MARK TWAIN

Retold by Diane Mowat

Who wants to live in a house, wear clean clothes, be good, and go to school every day? Not young Huckleberry Finn, that's for sure.

So Huck runs away, and is soon floating down the great Mississippi River on a raft. With him is Jim, a black slave who is also running away. But life is not always easy for the two friends.

And there's 300 dollars waiting for anyone who catches poor Jim . . .